Mother and Baby Verreaux's Sifaka

Books in the Wildlife of the World series:

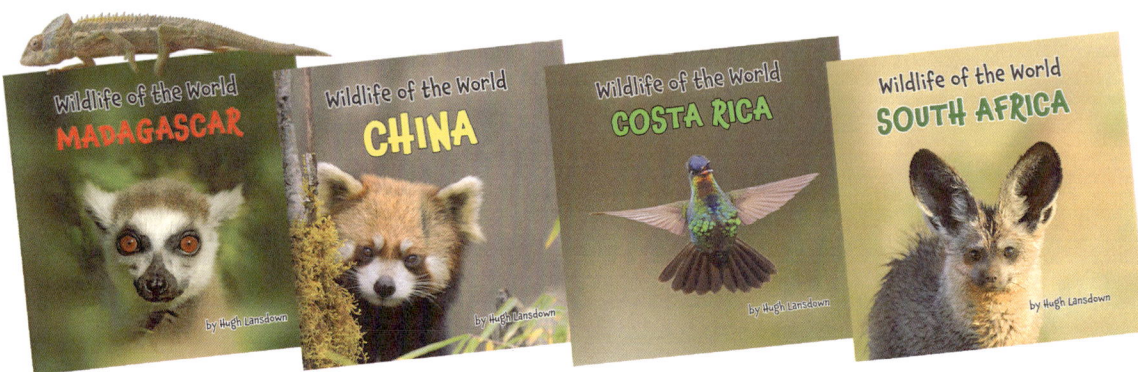

Wildlife of the World: Madagascar
Wildlife of the World: China
Wildlife of the World: Costa Rica
Wildlife of the World: South Africa

Coming soon:
Wildlife of the World: Japan

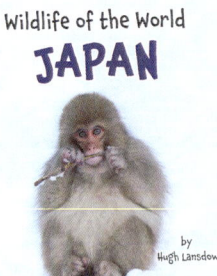

Visit *www.wildlifeoftheworld.com* to find out more about the books in the Wildlife of the World series.

Wildlife of the World

Madagascar

by

Hugh Lansdown

Text copyright © Hugh Lansdown 2024
Photography copyright © Hugh Lansdown 2024
All rights reserved.
ISBN: 978-1-917175-01-2

Hugh Lansdown has asserted his right under the Copyright, Designs and Patent Act 1988 to be identified as the author of this work.

This book is meant to be educational, informative and entertaining. Although the author and publisher have made every effort to ensure that the information in this book was correct at the time of publication, the author and publisher do not assume and hereby disclaim any liability to any party for loss, damage or disruption caused by errors or omissions, whether such errors or omissions result from negligence, accident or any other cause.

The names given to animals in the book and associated online media are the most appropriate English names the author was able to find based on visible characteristics. They don't represent a precise scientific identification, which in many cases would require the animal to be captured and a detailed examination carried out.

First published 2024
by Natural Planet Books
Unit 134893
PO Box 7169
Poole
BH15 9EL

www.naturalplanetbooks.com

Library Cataloguing in Publication Data. A catalogue record for this book is available from the British Library.

All rights reserved. No part of this book may be reprinted or reproduced or utilised in any form or by electronic, mechanical or any other means, now known or hereafter invented, including photocopying or recording, or in any information storage or retrieval system, without the permission in writing from the publisher.

How to use this book

This is an 'Interactive' book, which means that as well as paper pages, it has digital ones containing videos, sound and slide-shows.

How do I access the digital pages?

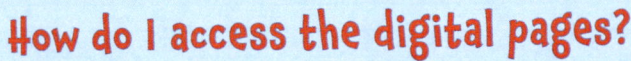

1 By scanning the QR codes

Throughout the book you will see Interactive Zones which look like this:

Just scan the black and white QR codes using a mobile phone, tablet or any device with a camera that can read QR codes.

2 By searching the Internet

If your device doesn't have a camera or you can't read QR codes, you can just search the Internet for:

- **Hugh Lansdown photography**
- then click on **Books**
- **Wildlife of the World: Madagascar**
- **Media Links**

You'll see a list of all the digital pages with the page number in this book that each one is linked to.

Wildlife Extras!

Some wildlife pages in this book have hidden animals that haven't been labelled. See how many you can spot and then check the list on page 48 to see if you got them

Contents

	Page
How to use this book	6
Map of Madagascar	8
Where is Madagascar?	9
Regions of Madagascar	10
Southern Spiny Forest	11
Eastern Rainforest	15
Central Highlands	19
Western Dry Forest	23
Wetlands	27
Iconic Madagascan Animals	30
Indri	32
Endemic Birds	34
Ring-tailed Lemurs	36
Chameleons	38
Mantellid Frogs	40
Hidden Wildlife Puzzle	42
Conserving Madagascar's Wildlife	44
Puzzle Answers	46
Wildlife Extras	48

See page 10 for an online interactive map of Madagascar

Madagascar

- Antsiranana
- Mahajanga
- Toamasina
- Antananarivo
- Antsirabe
- Fianarantsoa
- Toliara
- Taolagnaro

Mozambique Channel

Indian Ocean

The African mainland ←

Asia →

Where is Madagascar?

Madagascar is the world's 4th largest island and lies in the Indian Ocean off the east coast of Africa. It used to be joined to India and Australia, but separated 90 million years ago, and since then has developed its own very special wildlife.

About 80% of the animals are endemic, which means they're found nowhere else in the world. This includes strange mammals like lemurs and tenrecs as well as many different types of birds, amphibians, reptiles and invertebrates.

Read on to learn about some of these incredible Madagascan creatures!

It's over here... in the Indian Ocean!

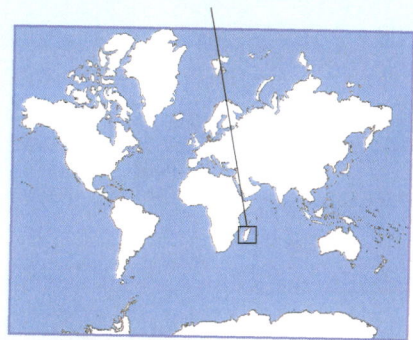

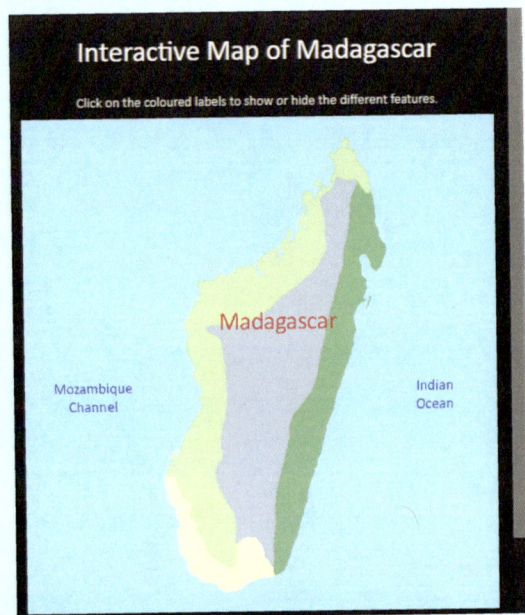

Regions of Madagascar

A line of mountains known as the Central Highlands runs down the centre of Madagascar, dividing the country into a number of different biological regions:

- **Southern Spiny Forest**
- **Eastern Rainforest**
- **Central Highlands**
- **Western Dry Forest**
- **Wetlands**

Try loading the **Interactive Map** and clicking the buttons to show the different regions. You can also see some major towns and cities and the national parks where many of the photos in this book were taken.

INTERACTIVE ZONE!

Scan the QR code to explore the interactive map

(If you're not sure how, check page 6 for details.)

Southern Spiny Forest

The south is the driest region of Madagascar and the only place in the world where endangered spiny forest is found... with its own unique wildlife. **Three-eyed lizards** get their name from the strange third eye on the back of their head, which scientists think is used to check the position of the sun!

Giant hissing cockroaches get their name from their huge size, and the loud, scary hissing noise they make if they're disturbed.

Three-eyed Lizard

Giant Hissing Cockroach

WHAT LIVES IN THE SPINY FOREST?

Since spiny forest isn't found anywhere else in the world, it's not really surprising that lots of special animals live there!

Ground rollers are a family of long-legged birds only found in Madagascar. They're not good at flying, but run extremely fast, hunting reptiles and large insects by chasing them through the undergrowth.

Soapberry bugs get their name because they feed on the seeds of soapberry plants. They can mate for as long as 24 hours at a time and are often seen coupled together on twigs and bushes.

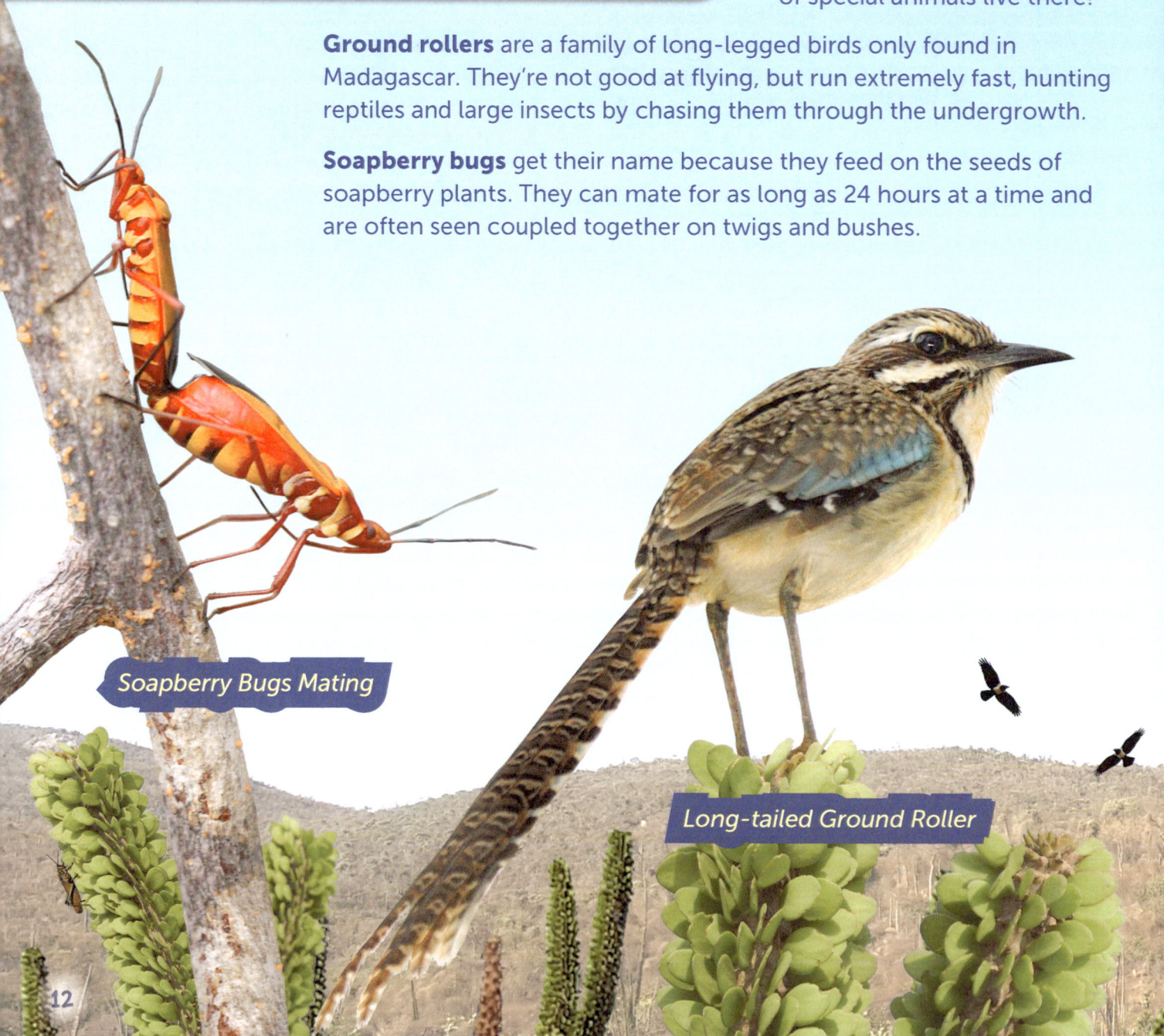

Soapberry Bugs Mating

Long-tailed Ground Roller

Jewel beetles are a beautiful group of insects with colourful wing cases, which in some parts of the world are made into jewellery.

Lemurs are a special family of mammals, only found in Madagascar. Their ancestors arrived from mainland Africa about 50 million years ago and since then they have evolved into over 100 different types. As you will see, they have all sorts of different shapes, sizes and lifestyles.

Cute **white-footed sportive lemurs** only live in the spiny forest, where they feed at night on the leaves and flowers of the weird spiny plants.

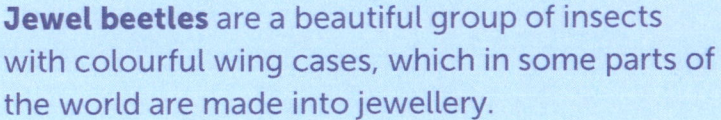
WHAT ARE THEY LIKE?

Jewel Beetle

White-footed Sportive Lemur

Dancing Sifakas!

Sifakas are a type of lemur that has evolved to live in the trees like monkeys. They have long back legs to help them leap from branch to branch, but this makes it difficult to walk on four legs... so instead they 'dance' across open ground!

Visit the Interactive Zone to watch sifakas in the spiny forest, or the **Interactive Map** on page 10 to see where the southern spiny forest is located.

INTERACTIVE ZONE!

Scan the QR code to watch sifakas 'dancing'

(If you're not sure how, check page 6 for details.)

Verreaux's Sifaka 'Dancing'

Eastern Rainforest

Madagascar's easterly winds pick water up from the Indian Ocean which falls as rain on the east of the country. This allows dense rainforest to grow which is full of wildlife, and being Madagascar, much of it is unique... like the pretty little **velvet asity** and the spiky **lowland streaked tenrec**.

Like lemurs, tenrecs are a family of mammals only found in Madagascar that have evolved into many different shapes and sizes. Although the lowland streaked tenrec looks like a strange, colourful hedgehog, it is actually more closely related to elephants!

Velvet Asity

Lowland Streaked Tenrec

WHAT LIVES IN THE RAINFOREST?

As the human population grows, people chop the rainforest down to plant crops and use the wood as fuel... which is very bad news for any animals that live there.

Nowhere in Madagascar has more endangered species than the eastern rainforest, including the strange-looking **Glaw's chameleon** and even stranger **giraffe weevils**. Male weevils use their long necks to fight each other for the best territory, while females use theirs to roll leaves up into little nests for their young.

Lemurs are officially the most endangered animals in the world, due to the loss of their habitat and being illegally hunted for food and the pet trade. Cute **eastern woolly lemurs** get their name from their thick, fluffy fur. They live in small family groups feeding on leaves and flowers at night, and like to sleep cuddled together during the day.

Glaw's Chameleon

Giraffe Weevil

HOW DO THEY LIVE THERE?

Eastern Woolly Lemurs

The strangest of all the lemurs, is the **aye-aye**, which has weird hands with different shaped fingers for different jobs!

The skinny third finger is used to investigate small holes in trees, while the big, powerful fourth finger can dig out grubs and the insides of tough fruit.

Aye-aye Hand

Aye-aye Feeding on Coconut

INTERACTIVE ZONE!

Scan the QR code to watch sifakas in the rainforest

(If you're not sure how, check page 6 for details.)

Rainforest Sifakas

Different regions of Madagascar have different types of sifaka, and the biggest and most colourful is the **diademed sifaka** in the eastern rainforest.

Visit the Interactive Zone to watch diademed sifakas, or the **Interactive Map** on page 10 to see where the eastern rainforest is located.

Diademed Sifaka

Central Highlands

The mountainous plateau running down the centre of Madagascar is where most of the country's 30 million people live. Originally, it was covered in forest, but most has been cut down to clear the land for building and crops.

Some wildlife still lives there, including beautiful **olive bee-eaters**, which eat all sorts of flying insects (not just bees!). **Bush cricket nymphs** can't fly, so they're safe from bee-eaters until they become adult and grow their first wings.

Bush Cricket Nymph

A Pair of Olive Bee-eaters

WHAT LIVES IN THE HIGHLANDS?

A surprising amount of wildlife is able to survive in the towns and farmland of the highlands. **Madagascar kestrels** eat all sorts of small animals including insects, birds, mammals and reptiles. They spot them while hovering or perched on a convenient twig... then suddenly swoop down to grab their prey.

The **Malagasy giant chameleon** is the largest chameleon in the world and can grow to nearly 70cm long. It is one of the few chameleons that can survive in villages and farmland where it feeds on large insects as well as small birds and other reptiles. It uses its impressive camouflage to ambush unsuspecting prey (see page 43).

Madagascar Kestrel

Malagasy Giant Chameleon

Lots of invertebrates live in the fields and gardens of the highlands.

Madagascar lynx spiders don't make webs, instead they use sharp eyesight and speed to hunt their prey... and also to keep out of the reach of predators like kestrels and chameleons!

Madagascar giant swallowtail butterflies have a different way of staying safe. Their caterpillars feed on the poisonous leaves of a vine, storing the poison in their bodies. This makes the butterflies poisonous too, so predators have to leave them alone!

HOW DO THEY SURVIVE THERE?

Madagascar Giant Swallowtail

Madagascar Lynx Spider

Highland Birdlife

Many different birds live in the highlands, like the **Madagascar paradise flycatcher** and **Malagasy brush warbler**, which feed on small insects and build their nests in hedges or small bushes. Others, like ducks and egrets, patrol areas of marsh and small lakes in search of food.

Visit the Interactive Zone to see some different highland birds, or the **Interactive Map** on page 10 to see where the Central Highlands are located.

Madagascar Paradise Flycatcher on its Nest

INTERACTIVE ZONE!

Scan the QR code for more birds from the Central Highlands

(If you're not sure how, check page 6 for details.)

Malagasy Brush Warbler Collecting Nesting Material

Western Dry Forest

By the time Madagascar's easterly winds have passed over the Central Highlands there is barely any rain left, so western forests are very dry, with their own special wildlife.

Red-fronted brown lemurs usually eat flowers, fruit and leaves, but they're also quite cheeky and will steal food from people if they get a chance! (See page 44).

Beautiful **giant day geckos** mainly hunt insects, but they also like the taste of a little fruit or nectar now and then.

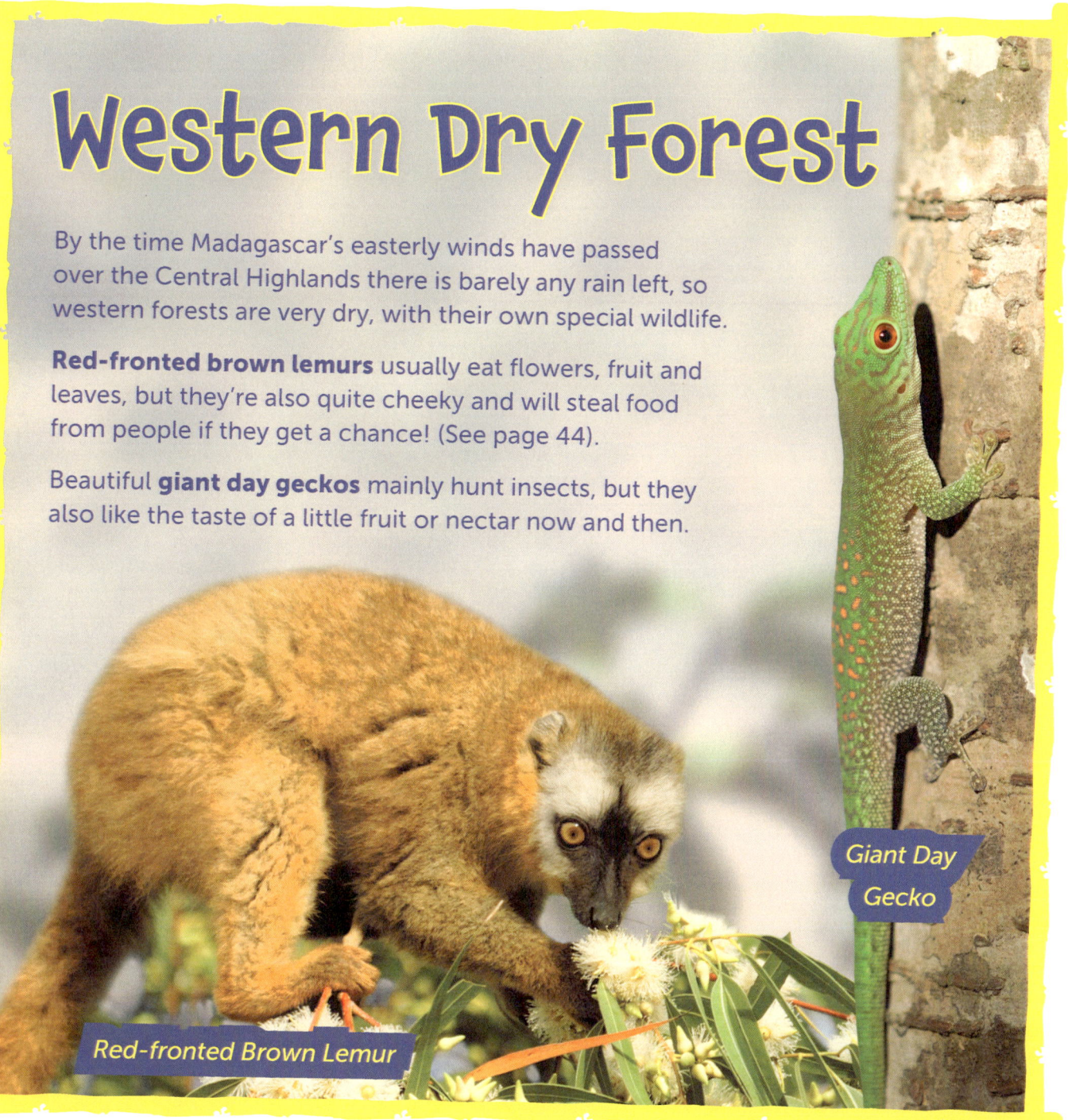

Giant Day Gecko

Red-fronted Brown Lemur

WHAT LIVES IN THE DRY FOREST?

Western Madagascar is a very rocky, dry region, so it's difficult to grow crops and not many people live there. As a result, a lot of the forest still survives, but with so little rain it grows quite slowly and there is no dense undergrowth for animals to hide in.

Northern big-eyed snakes live in the dry leaf litter on the forest floor, where they hunt lizards, frogs and sometimes even other snakes!

Madagascar paradise flycatchers like to chase insects through the forest. There are two different colour forms: the beautiful silvery white one on this page and also the deep orange form on page 22.

Madagascar Paradise Flycatcher

Northern Big-eyed Snake

HOW ARE THEY SO DIFFERENT?

Gray Mouse Lemur

It's hard to believe the two mammals on this page are closely related, but they are actually both lemurs.

Mouse lemurs are the smallest primates in the world. They are tiny, secretive creatures that race around the treetops at night in search of small insects and fruit to eat. Sifakas on the other hand are huge, powerful primates active in the daytime. They live in noisy groups and eat a strictly vegetarian diet.

Both the **gray mouse lemur** and **Coquerel's sifaka** are only found in Madagascar's dry forests, where they are endangered by habitat loss and illegal hunting.

Coquerel's Sifaka

Strange Waxy Bugs!

There are many strange animals in Madagascar, but surely **flatid bug larvae** must be the weirdest!

The adults are fairly normal bugs like the green one on the left, but the larvae look nothing like their parents. They are white, with long legs and weird waxy tendrils sticking out of their backs.

Visit the Interactive Zone to learn more about flatid bugs, or try the **Interactive Map** on page 10 to see where the western dry forest is located.

Adult Flatid Bug with Larvae

Flatid Bug Larva

INTERACTIVE ZONE!

Scan the QR code to watch flatid bug behaviour

(If you're not sure how, check page 6 for details.)

Wetlands

With much of the country being so dry, wetland areas like rivers, lakes and marshes are an important home for all sorts of different animals.

Scary-looking **Madagascar forest crayfish** are a sort of lobster that live in eastern forest streams, while beautiful **Madagascar kingfishers** hunt tiny fish in wetlands all over the country.

Madagascar Kingfisher Eating a Fish

Madagascar Forest Crayfish

WHAT LIVES IN THE WETLANDS?

The **Madagascar fish eagle** is one of the world's rarest birds, with only about 240 left alive. They all live in Madagascar's northern wetlands, where they hunt large fish by swooping down and plucking them out of the water with their strong talons.

Pretty **squacco herons**, on the other hand, are common marshland birds that feed on frogs and insects all over Madagascar and many other parts of Africa.

Madagascar Fish Eagle

Squacco Heron

Powder-blue Reed Frog

Lots of different insects live in wetland areas, including many types of dragonfly. Smaller ones like this **red damselfly** are food for beautiful **powder-blue reed frogs,** which live on the shores of lakes and rivers in eastern Madagascar.

Madagascar's increasing droughts are a big problem for many wetland animals, but not for birds such as **white-faced whistling ducks** and **red-billed teal**. Like the squacco heron, they are common throughout the island, but if the wetlands where they live dry up they'll just fly off to find a new one, sometimes even as far as the African mainland!

HOW DO THEY SURVIVE THERE?

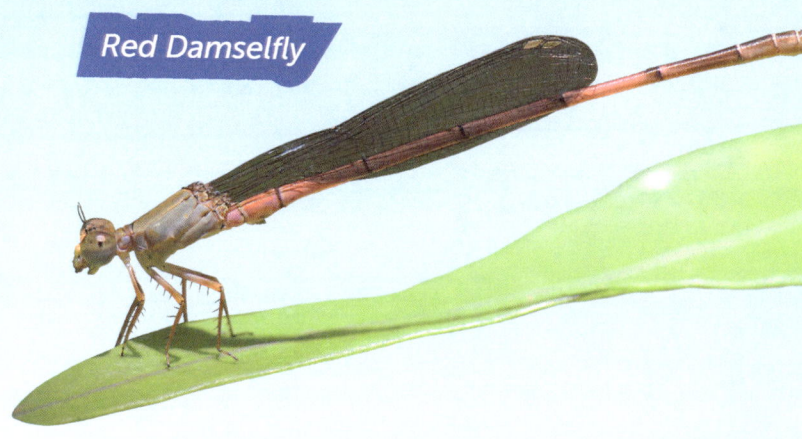

Red Damselfly

Red-billed Teal

White-faced Whistling Ducks

Iconic Madagascan Animals

Madagascar has so many amazing animals that it's almost impossible to pick out the most iconic ones... but I've chosen five groups that I think are extra special. You can find more information about them on the next few pages:

- **Indri**
- **Endemic Birds**
- **Ring-tailed Lemurs**
- **Chameleons**
- **Mantellid Frogs**

Ring-tailed Lemur

Mantellid Jumping Frog

Indri

Indri are the biggest of all the lemurs and the only ones that don't have a visible tail. They live in the eastern rainforest and are critically endangered due to their forest home being cut down for fuel and to grow crops.

Many Madagascan people think indri are sacred, and some old stories say they are descended from people who got lost in the forest many years ago. One reason for this is their strange, wailing call, which echoes through the forest... and sounds a bit like people crying. (Check it out in the Interactive Zone!)

Indri live in small family groups with a male, a female and several young of different ages. As with many types of lemur, the adult female is the group leader.

They are active during the day and have a completely vegetarian diet, with the group moving through the treetops together in search of leaves, fruits and flowers to eat.

With their staring yellow eyes, bright red mouth and creepy, wailing cries, it's easy to see why some people believe indri have supernatural powers!

Visit the **Interactive Zone** to watch indri in the rainforest and listen to their strange call.

INTERACTIVE ZONE!

Scan the QR code to watch indri in the rainforest

(If you're not sure how, check page 6 for details.)

Endemic Birds

There are about 250 different native birds in Madagascar and nearly half, including five whole families, are endemic... meaning they are found nowhere else in the world.

The **subdesert mesite** is a member of a strange family of highly endangered birds that can barely fly. They live in small groups in the spiny forest, where all the members share a single nest and the job of incubating eggs and feeding the young.

Subdesert Mesite

Crested Coua

Couas are large, colourful relatives of cuckoos, and **vangas** are small forest birds that started as a single species but have since evolved into many different types.

Vasa parrots shed their feathers during the nesting season, and some females end up with completely bald heads!

Visit the **Interactive Zone** to learn more about Madagascar's endemic birds and how they live.

Lesser Vasa Parrot

Hook-billed Vanga

INTERACTIVE ZONE!

Scan the QR code to see more endemic birds

(If you're not sure how, check page 6 for details.)

Ring-tailed Lemurs

With their cute black eye-patches, red eyes and long black-and-white tail, **ring-tailed lemurs** are probably the most famous of all the lemurs. You can see them in zoos all over the world, as well as in books and on TV, and they are also popular as cuddly toys.

Feeding

Sunbathing

They live in large groups of 30 or more in southern dry and spiny forests, and are active during the day. Each morning when they wake up, the first thing they do is spend half an hour sunbathing to get warm!

Then they wander off in search of food, walking with their long tails held high in the air like black-and-white flags. This acts as a signal to the rest of the group so they all know exactly where the others are.

Visit the **Interactive Zone** to watch some wild ring-tailed lemurs.

Signalling

INTERACTIVE ZONE!

Scan the QR code to see more ring-tailed lemurs

(If you're not sure how, check page 6 for details.)

Chameleons

Brown Leaf Chameleon

Chameleons are a very strange, special type of lizard, and over half the world's species are only found in Madagascar. They are famous for being able to change their colour, but also have weird eyes on rotating turrets and a tongue they can fire at prey like a missile!

Sometimes, chameleons change their colour to camouflage themselves, but more often it's to show what mood they're in. Most are green or brown when relaxed, but change to black or bright red if they're angry or frightened!

Carpet Chameleon

A chameleon's tongue is extremely long and can be twice the length of its body. It's so long they have to keep it rolled up in their mouth like a hose! They fire it at insect prey, which stick to the end and are then dragged back into the chameleon's mouth. It all happens in a fraction of a second, which is much too fast for the insects to see it coming!

Visit the **Interactive Zone** to see more chameleons and learn how they use their strange eyes.

Lance-nosed Chameleon

Parson's Chameleon

INTERACTIVE ZONE!

Scan the QR code to see more chameleons

(If you're not sure how, check page 6 for details.)

Mantellid Frogs

Green Bright-eyed Frog

Madagascar Bright-eyed Frog

Believe it or not, all these frogs are all closely related members of the same family!

There are an incredible 300 different types of frog in Madagascar, and none of them are found anywhere else in the world. Most belong to the mantellid family and, like the lemurs, are all descended from a single ancestor but over thousands of years have developed into many different shapes and sizes.

The **bright-eyed frogs** have evolved to hunt in trees at night, with suckers on their fingers to help them climb and huge eyes to see in the dark.

East Betsileo Madagascar frogs, on the other hand, are superbly adapted to life on the forest floor, with little spines and ridges to help them blend into the leaf litter (see pages 42 and 46).

The tiny little **pandanus frog** has found a different home altogether. It lives in the tiny gap between the leaves of pandanus plants and even lays its eggs in the rainwater that collects there!

Pandanus Frog

East Betsileo Madagascar Frog

Hidden Wildlife Puzzle!

Many of Madagascar's animals have clever camouflage to keep themselves hidden and safe from predators.

Can you spot the 7 animals on these two pages? (Answers on page 46.)

Conserving Madagascar's Wildlife

WHAT ARE THE PROBLEMS?

Burning forest to clear the land for crops

Madagascar probably has the most unique and unusual wildlife of any country in the world... but unfortunately it is also some of the most endangered.

As one of the world's poorest countries, many Madagascan people can't afford to buy food, so sometimes they catch wild animals to eat or sell as pets.

People also cut down forests so they can plant crops for food. The trees can be made into charcoal for cooking and to heat their homes.

Some forests and crops are also dying due to drought, which is becoming more and more common with global warming.

Charcoal for sale

Brown lemurs eating food people have left out

HOW CAN THEY BE FIXED?

Dried-up rice paddy fields due to drought

If we want Madagascar's wildlife to be protected, we need to help the people find ways to survive that don't harm it.

One way is to pay local guides to show us the wildlife in Madagascar's ancient forests, instead of viewing animals that are kept captive, away from their natural habitat.

Another way is donating money to charities that employ local people to study animals and protect their habitats, which supports the communities where they live.

Hopefully, if the people of Madagascar and the rest of the world all work together, we can keep this magical island's amazing wildlife safe, now and into the future.

Captive fossa

Houses made of mud and brushwood

Answers

to the hidden wildlife puzzle on page 42.

1 Stick Mantid

This little praying mantis rests disguised as a stick during the day, then comes out at night to hunt.

2 Orange Underwing Moth

This moth has bright orange on its underwings to signal to other moths, but keeps it hidden when resting so predators can't see it.

3 East Betsileo Madagascar Frog

This frog lives amongst leaf litter in the rainforest and has lots of strange ridges and spines sticking out of its body to make it look like a pile of sticks and dead leaves. (You can see another photo on page 41.)

Hidden Wildlife Puzzle!

Many of Madagascar's animals have clever camouflage to keep themselves hidden and safe from predators.

Can you spot the 7 animals on these two pages? (Answers on page 46.)

4 Adult Madagascar Nightjar

This bird is a female nightjar sitting in the leaf litter of the southern spiny forest... but she's not alone!

7 Giant Leaf-tailed Gecko

Leaf-tailed geckos have some of the best camouflage of any animal in the world... and are sometimes impossible to see even when you're looking straight at them!

Below is a close-up of the head. If you look closely you might be able to see its eye and mouth as well as some toes on the left leg.

5 Madagascar Nightjar chick

This is the nightjar's chick sitting next to its parent. (In fact, there is another chick hiding under their feathers!)

6 Malagasy Giant Chameleon

This chameleon is disguised to look just like the broken branch it's clinging to. (You can see another on page 20.)

Wildlife Extras!

On some pages, there are photos of animals that haven't been labelled, usually in the background or hidden in vegetation.

See how many you can spot, then check the list below to see if you got them all. You can also scan the QR code above to find out more about them.

Page	Animals
9	Two great egrets in the paddy field, and a cattle egret flying above.
12	A rainbow milkweed locust sitting on a plant in the bottom left, and two pied crows flying behind the long-tailed ground roller.
13	A pied crow flying in the background behind the lemur.
15	An assassin bug on a leaf just below the asity.
18	A common newtonia perched on a branch behind the sifaka.
19	Two olive bee-eaters flying in the background.
20	A yellow-billed kite flying behind the chameleon's nose.
21	A yellow-billed kite flying behind the giant swallowtail, and a tent-web spider on the plant in the bottom right.
24	A Gravenhorst's mabuya lizard on the left behind the snake.
27	An Ambrana Madagascar frog on a stone in the bottom right.
28	A squacco heron flying behind the one that's perched on a branch, and three white-faced whistling ducks flying behind the frog.
29	Three white-faced whistling ducks flying behind the teal.
34	An acraea butterfly perched on the plant in the bottom left.

Photographing Wildlife in Madagascar

I'm a wildlife photographer and I travel the world, exploring wild, remote places in search of some of the amazing animals that live there. I'm not interested in photographing captive animals in places like zoos and wildlife parks... but in Madagascar the difference isn't always clear!

Madagascar is a very poor country and there are some people there who struggle to afford food to eat and clothes to wear. The money they earn by showing tourists the country's amazing wildlife could decide whether they have a meal to eat or can send their children to school.

Because of this, local people sometimes catch wild animals like lemurs and chameleons and move them out of their natural habitat to places where it's easy for tourists to see them. These animals are often given food to encourage them to stay, or put somewhere like an island where it's hard for them to leave. They seem to be wild animals, but they aren't really... because they're not living in their natural home and they depend on people looking after them for their survival.

For this book I considered an animal to be 'wild' if it was living in its natural habitat, was free to come and go, and was not dependent on people for its daily survival (for example by feeding it).

Hugh Lansdown

Index

Acraea Butterfly 34, 48
Ambrana Madagascar Frog 27, 48
Assassin Bug 15, 48
Aye-aye 17
Beetles 13, 16
Brown-leaf Chameleon 38
Brown Lemurs 23, 44
Bugs 12, 15, 26, 48
Bush Cricket 19
Butterflies 21, 34, 48
Camouflage 20, 42–43, 46–47
Carpet Chameleon 38
Cattle Egret 9, 48
Central Highlands 19–22
Chabert Vanga 31
Chameleons 16, 20, 31, 38–39, 43, 47, 55
Common Newtonia 18, 48
Conservation 44–45
Coquerel's Sifaka 25
Couas 34–35
Crested Coua 34

Diademed Sifaka 18
Drought 29, 44–45
Dry Forest 23–26
East Betsileo Frog 41, 42, 46
Eastern Woolly Lemur 16–17
Endemic Birds 12, 15, 22, 28, 30–31, 34–35
Flatid Bug 26
Frogs & Toads 27–30, 40–42, 46, 48
Giant Day Gecko 23
Giant Hissing cockroach 11
Giant Leaf-tailed Gecko 43, 47
Giraffe Weevil 16
Glaw's Chameleon 16
Gravenhorst's Mabuya 24, 48
Gray Mouse Lemur 25
Great Egret 9, 48
Green Bright-eyed Frog 40
Hook-billed Vanga 35
Indri 31–33
Jewel Beetle 13
Lance-nosed Chameleon 39, 55

Lemurs 1, 13, 14, 16–18, 23, 25, 30–33, 36–37, 44
Lesser Vasa Parrot 35
Lizards 11, 23, 24, 43, 47, 48
Long-tailed Ground Roller 12
Lowland Streaked Tenrec 15
Madagascar Bright-eyed Frog 40
Madagascar Fish Eagle 28
Madagascar Forest Crayfish 27
Madagascar Giant Swallowtail 21
Madagascar Kestrel 20
Madagascar Kingfisher 27
Madagascar Lynx Spider 21
Madagascar Nightjar 42–43, 46–47
Madagascar Paradise Flycatcher 22, 24
Malagasy Brush Warbler 22
Malagasy Giant Chameleon 20, 43, 47
Mantellid Frogs 27, 30, 40–42, 46
Mating 12
Northern Big-eyed Snake 24
Olive Bee-eater 19, 48
Orange Underwing Moth 42, 46
Pandanus Frog 41
Parson's Chameleon 31, 39
Pied Crow 12–13, 48

Powder-blue Reed Frog 28–29
Rainbow Milkweed Locust 12, 48
Rainforest 15–18, 32
Red-billed Teal 29
Red Damselfly 29
Red-fronted Brown Lemur 23
Ring-tailed Lemur 30, 36–37, 49
Sifaka 1, 14, 18, 25
Soapberry Bug 12
Spiders 21, 48
Spiny Forest 11–14, 34, 37
Squacco Heron 28, 48
Stick Mantid 42, 46
Subdesert Mesite 34
Tenrecs 15
Tent-web Spider 21, 48
Three-eyed Lizard 11
Vangas 31, 35
Velvet Asity 15
Verreaux's Sifaka 1, 14
Wetlands 27–29
White-faced Whistling Duck 28–29, 48
White-footed Sportive Lemur 13
Yellow-billed Kite 20–21, 48

About the Author

Hugh Lansdown is a Welsh wildlife photographer who has travelled extensively, and his images have appeared in hundreds of books, magazines and other publications across the globe.

He is also heavily involved in conservation at home in Wales, working for local wildlife charities, carrying out habitat management work and giving talks about wildlife conservation.

You can find out more about Hugh's photography, writing and conservation work by visiting his website or signing up to his monthly newsletters:

www.hughlansdown.com/newsletters.html

Acknowledgements

Many people have helped me with my photography in Madagascar, and with the writing of this book. I would like to thank some of them here:

Brett Massoud and Huguette Marevaka of Dadamanga Travel for their brilliant organisation of my second trip to Madagascar.

Didi Razafimahaleo for driving me around the country and keeping me safe!

Klaus Sperling of Roadhouse Sarl for organising my first trip to explore Madagascar, and Alain for driving me around.

Lambert Dimilahy for guiding me around Berenty.

Fano Radad for guiding me around Antananarivo.

Tina Heritianasylvana for guiding me around Andasibe-Mantadia.

Ellie Owen at Rowanvale for her astute, invaluable advice.

All photos, video clips and sound recordings of wildlife in this book and on the associated web pages were taken by Hugh Lansdown in Madagascar, except the fossa on page 45 which Hugh photographed in Tokyo Ueno Zoo.

All other animals were wild and free (as explained on page 49) except: the tenrec on page 15, which had been captured by some local villagers and was released into the wild after the photo was taken, and the aye-aye on page 17, which was living in its natural habitat on a small island, but was unable to leave and dependent on food provided by local people each day.

Sneaky Animals!

A few random animals seem to have sneaked into the book when Hugh wasn't looking...

Page 2   - a warty chameleon

Page 3   - a ring-tailed lemur

Page 5   - three Verreaux's sifakas, two adults and a baby

Page 6   - a giraffe weevil and an African wood white butterfly

Page 7   - a Madagascar flying fox

Page 50 - a crab spider

Page 54 - a giant day gecko

What did you think of Wildlife of the World - Madagascar?

A big thank you for buying this book. It means a lot that you chose this book specifically from such a wide range on offer.

We do hope you enjoyed it.

Book reviews are incredibly important for an author. All feedback helps them improve their writing for future projects and for developing this edition. If you are able to spare a few minutes to post a review on Amazon or Goodreads, that would be much appreciated.

Female Lance-nosed Chameleon

www.ingramcontent.com/pod-product-compliance
Lightning Source LLC
Chambersburg PA
CBRC100224100526
44591CB00007B/61